THE *featured* Violinist
Made Easy!

Published by
Chester Music Limited
8/9 Frith Street, London, W1D 3JB, England.

Exclusive distributors:
Music Sales Limited
Distribution Centre, Newmarket Road,
Bury St Edmunds, Suffolk, IP33 3YB, England.

Music Sales Pty Limited
120 Rothschild Avenue, Rosebery, NSW 2018, Australia.

Order No. CH70532   ISBN 1-84609-208-6

This book © Copyright 2006 Wise Publications,
a division of Music Sales Limited.

Edited by Rebecca Taylor.
Printed in the EU.
www.musicsales.com

FREE piano accompaniments and
audio backing tracks available online.
Visit: www.featuredseries.com
Registration is free and easy.
Your registration code is: SC075

Chester Music
part of The Music Sales Group
London / New York / Paris / Sydney / Copenhagen / Berlin / Madrid / Tokyo

My Heart That Believest

Music by Johann Sebastian Bach

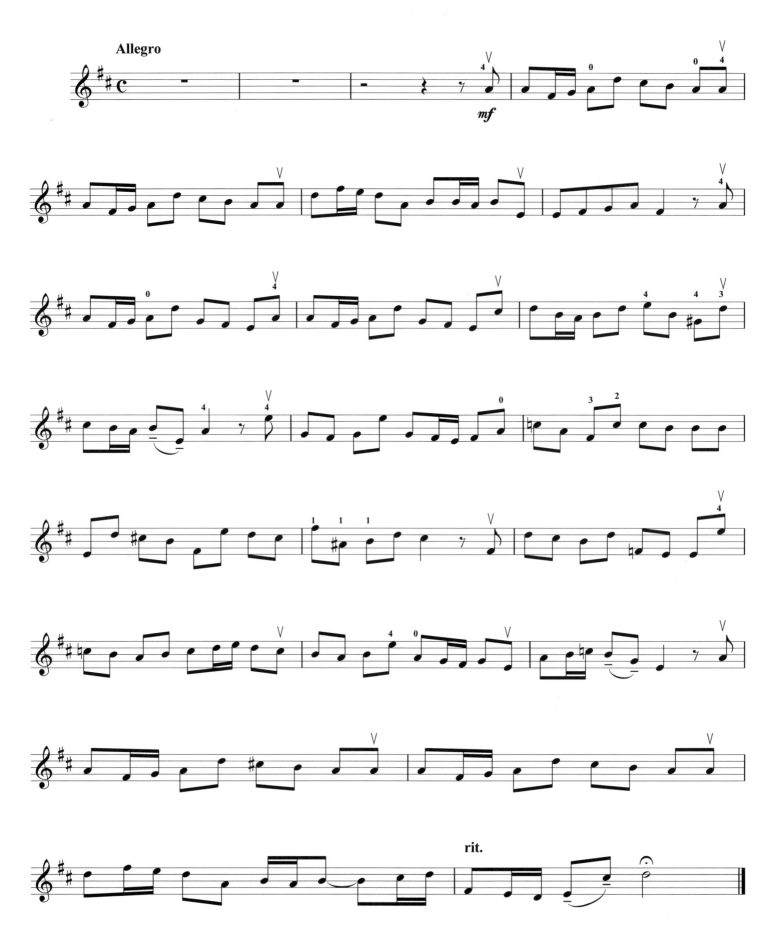

Moonlight Sonata

Music by Ludwig Van Beethoven

Waltz

Music by Johannes Brahms

Valse

Music by Léo Delibes

Solveig's Song

Music by Edward Grieg

Andante con moto

To Spring

Music by Edward Grieg

Arioso

Music by George Frederic Handel

Largo

Music by George Frederic Handel

Meditation

Music by Jules Massenet

Andante

Music by Felix Mendelssohn

Themes From
Eine Kleine Nachtmusik

Music by Wolfgang Amadeus Mozart

Träumerei

Music by Robert Schumann

Emperor Waltz

Music by Joseph Strauss

La Donna É Mobile

Music by Guiseppe Verdi

Andante Cantabile

Music by Pyotr Ilyich Tchaikovsky

Spring

Music by Antonio Vivaldi

21

Autumn

Music by Antonio Vivaldi

Winter

Music by Antonio Vivaldi

La Paloma

Music by Sebastien Yradier

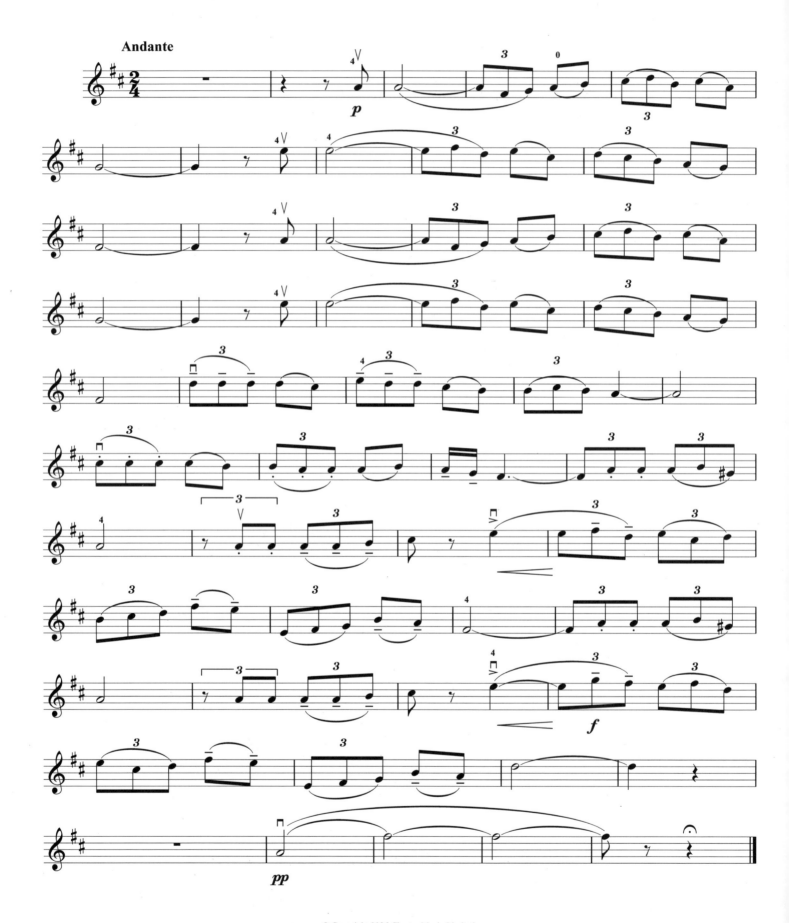